Ruby and Garbie

by

Doris Westbrook

DORRANCE
PUBLISHING CO
EST. 1920
PITTSBURGH, PENNSYLVANIA 15238

Dorrance Publishing Co
585 Alpha Drive
Suite 103
Pittsburgh, PA 15238
Visit our website at *www.dorrancebookstore.com*

ISBN: 978-1-4809-9121-7
eISBN: 978-1-4809-9097-5

In honor and love to my mother, Ruby Garber Herrington.

This story is written and dedicated in the memory of Ruby Garber Herrington. There have been numerous articles printed about the love of animals by elderly people. This story is about that kind of shared love between Ruby and Garbie. But first, I must tell you some things about Ruby.

Ruby came from a heritage she was proud to share with others. She was married to the same man, James Monroe Herrington, for over thirty years. Ruby became a widow at the age of fifty-six and never remarried. She died at the age of ninety-one. Ruby was survived by a son, daughter, four granddaughters, and two sisters at the time of her death in November 1988. After working for the State of Texas, posting oil productions for eleven years following her husband's death, she retired and moved to Meridian, Texas, a small, quiet town near Waco. There she had numerous friends at church, garden club, and the Forty-two Club. To keep from being lonely, she often made a dessert to take to a sick friend. Many summers Ruby would bake cookies for the children attending Vacation Bible School at the First Baptist Church. More than likely, the balanced meals she prepared for herself and the rest she got contributed to her longevity. She spent many hours doing needlework, reading, and watching TV. She was well versed on current events. There was another factor that most likely contributed to five more years to her life, and that was her "Beautiful Angel" (the first name she gave her Weimaraner puppy), which she received in November 1981. She was officially named Garber Girl—Garbie for short. So, here is the story about Ruby and Garbie.

Ruby's daughter and her family had seven Weimaraner puppies born to Charlotte, their mother, in June 1981. Having sold all of the puppies except the runt of the litter, Ruby's son-in-law approached her with the idea of keeping this cute runt of a dog until Christmas just to see if she might like having a dog for company and protection on her large piece of property in Meridian. She agreed to have the dog brought down at Thanksgiving with the understanding that if she didn't want to keep the dog, she could give it back to her family when she visited for the Christmas holidays. By the time Christmas came, she was in love with the runt she called "Angel." Ruby was already so attached to her Garbie that she had to let us know that she thought her dog was smarter than Charlotte and much prettier than Charlotte.

When Ruby and Garbie returned to Meridian after Christmas, there was no question that Garbie had found her home with Ruby. Garbie enjoyed being outdoors and running in her large yard. When Ruby went outside, Garbie seemed to sense that she was an older person and did not try to jump up on her. A doghouse was built by some dear friends right outside Ruby's bedroom window on a small porch. Every night before Ruby retired, she would shine her flashlight on Garbie to see if she was in bed. Needless to say, Garbie was spoiled. Ruby put ice cubes in Garbie's water bowl in the summertime and made gravy for her supper many evenings. The love for this dog gave Ruby a purpose for getting out of bed in the mornings. She had a renewed interest in life because of her new responsibility. Garbie needed Ruby just as Ruby needed Garbie. Ruby would pet Garbie at the fence when she would get the paper and mail every morning. Garbie would cry when Ruby would go into the house.

After Ruby moved to the nursing home, Ruby's neighbors said that Garbie wailed outside Ruby's bedroom window for a week. Before Ruby died, some neighbors took Garbie to Ruby's outside window at the nursing home so Garbie could see Ruby and Ruby was able to see Garbie, which pleased both. The day of Ruby's funeral, Garbie never barked at people coming and going from Ruby's house, but instead she displayed a lovingly sad look that seemed to say, "I've lost my best friend."

The following excerpts are from Ruby's delightfully entertaining letters written to her family about her Angel Garbie:

Tonight when Angel was eating her supper, I thought it was a good time to put the straw back in her bed that she had pulled out. She came up behind me and wiped her mouth on the seat of my clean slacks. Then she ran back to her supper. She is so cute when I say, "No-no," and shake my head. She shakes her head "no-no." When I tell her how beautiful she is, she gets such a pleased expression on her face and turns her head and looks at me so cute.

I'm having Garbie a house made. I asked several people before I found a man who said he would make it. I hope I get it before bad weather comes again. However, she seems to like her bed and fared fine. When I went out to put the garbage can out front this P.M., she came around to see what I was doing. She thought I was leaving, and she just cried until she saw I was coming back.

Garbie and I are fine. I talked to Margie and George, and they came over in the rain. We planned from my bedroom windows how he could make a "shed" where her bed is. He can't do anything until the weather clears. One morning she was still asleep and I watched her awaken. She sat up and looked all around and started yawning. She did this several times. She is so cute and smart.

Well George came today and built Garbie's house. She

just loves it. She wouldn't go in it until after supper. I came in here to watch her from my window, and she was in it. It had rained several times in her bed, so the straw in the bottom was wet. This is so comfortable. On days when the sun is shining, she sits out in the sun and goes to sleep. She reminds me of myself in church when I go to sleep. When you awaken, you kinda jump.

Garbie is growing so fast—she looks like she is almost as big as her mother. I made her a skillet of gravy and put some bread in it. Then I gave her two cups of her Puppy Chow in water and her pill in cheese for her supper.

This Garbie is something else. She had a golf ball in her mouth trying to swallow it. Finally, she gave up and I went out and got that ball and put it in the waste basket. I was so afraid she would choke.

Garbie sends her love to you all.

Garbie is still so playful. I hardly dare go in the yard. Old age will slow her down.

Garbie is still just too smart!

I haven't washed but once and I really liked it (Ruby's new washing machine). The Woolite makes a lot of soap suds. So this Garbie goes out and plays in it, eats it, gets it all over her face and slaps it with her foot. That isn't all she has done, but I don't have time to write it all for I'm on my way to get my hair done.

Garbie had a good time in the wash water this A.M. She

dug a hole and got mud up to her knees.

I don't have time to tell you anything about Garbie. Sometimes she is good and sometimes she isn't. I don't know what to feed her since her birthday. The vet said to give her 2 of the heartworm pills now. I didn't ask him about what to feed her. I knew you would know.

One night Garbie barked so much before bedtime. I looked out and couldn't see anything, so I turned the yard light on and she still barked. Soon after I went to bed, she settled down. Next morning, she was still asleep on that piece of carpet out in the yard. It wasn't a cold night. I decided she was afraid she wouldn't hear whatever it was if she slept in her house. Just did that one night.

I love that Garbie—she gets sweeter all the time. I had some dry butter beans, so I cooked some for us. She really liked them. I gave her about a cup of them with three cups Purina Puppy Chow. She is always hungry.

Garbie is sitting out in the sun—she finds a good place and sits there and starts "nodding" but before she takes her nap she looks all around. I looked in the dogs for sale section of the *Dallas News* several times and there were not any of her kind listed. I'm going to the "Locker Plant" and get her some bones, then maybe she will quit trying to eat sticks. I guess it's natural because I read this article where their dog ate holes in the walls of their house. I don't know much about dogs, but I'm learning.

I went with Alice Long out to see her sister. When we got back, somehow Garbie didn't recognize me and she barked, backed off and came at me again. I was glad a fence was between us. When she saw it was me, she looked ashamed and came and was friendly.

Well, Garbie is trying to be good. When I pet her at the fence, she wants to play but she tries to bite my hand. I tell her, "No, no! We don't bite." She gets down and looks so sad, then I say, "Well, howdy do!" and she comes up smiling and shakes hands with me. She is so smart. I leave the gate open to the big back yard and she runs all over it.

Garbie is so sweet. She is growing so fast. I'm giving her eight cups of Puppy Chow a day, plus gravy, scraps from the table and brown beans. I let some beans get old, so I cooked them for her. She just loves them. She cries when I go to the mailbox.

Last Friday, Julio Martinez mowed my big backyard. Garbie didn't bark at him but I thought it was best to put her in the little yard. After he left, I opened the gate and was going to use a wire to keep it open. I had put the wire on the ground to get the leaves and stuff out of the way. So when I got ready for the wire, it was gone. I told Garbie I had to have that wire. What did she do with it? She just smiled and jumped around so pleased. I told her I would go to the garage and get another wire, which I did, and was slow. The wire was stiff. I looked down at my feet, and she had brought it back to me. I was so busy I didn't see where she had hid it.

I'm glad you told me Garbie makes funny noises in her sleep. She really does. I would have thought there was something the matter with her.

I called the vet to come and give Garbie her Parvo shot. He said he didn't make calls for small animals, said he couldn't do that much business. So I'll get Mike or Rodney Rich to go with me to take her to him. She is so sweet. She is eating ten cups of Puppy Chow a day. I hope that is enough.

Garbie is so sweet. I gave her a clean white rag to play with and when I looked about her later, the yard looked like we had snow—the rag was in such little pieces. This P.M. a man knocked on my front door and before I could get to the door, she was really barking. She couldn't see him. I don't know how she knew he was there.

When I told Alice Long the vet couldn't come to my house to give Garbie her booster shot for Parvo, she said she would come and help me take her out there to the vet in her station wagon. You don't say no to Alice. I wish I had a movie of us getting her in that strange car. I finally got in and she started to get in, then stopped. I pulled her front feet in and Alice pushed her back sides in. She got real close to me. When we got out there, she wouldn't go ahead of me—she felt better near me. The vet was busy, so his nurse gave her the shot. We had to put her on the table and she wouldn't get off. We had to lift her off. I told the nurse I wanted Dr. Metzger to see her, so he came in and he really complimented her. I told him to see if she has any fleas or ticks, etc. He looked her over good all the time petting her and said whatever you are doing, keep on, for she is just fine. Until I talked to people, I didn't realize how important this shot is. Last summer there was an epidemic here and a number of dogs died. She is so sweet and smart.

Not much to write about but Garbie. She "pouts" with me when I do something she doesn't like. Because there was a program I wanted to see on tonight, I fed her earlier than usual and when the show was over, I didn't go back and tell her good night and how beautiful she is, etc. Next morning she wasn't glad to see me, really looked sick or mad, didn't wag her tail. So I set her food down. She smelled it and went off and sat down. I came in my bedroom to watch her, and she rushed over to her food and ate it all. Last Saturday, I again picked up all that <u>stuff</u> she brings in her yard, including the piece of carpet which she just loves. It was all to pieces and dusty, and she would sling it and run and try to catch it. She pouted for about two days each time. But she always ate her food, so I knew she was alright.

Garbie went straight to her house after you left and slept all afternoon. She was tired. She and Charlotte were not still for a minute hardly. She looks like she is gaining some weight she lost. They just exercised too much for her. But she enjoyed it all, I'm sure.

Garbie didn't show any signs of missing you after you were gone. She went to her favorite place near the house in the shade and went to sleep. She was so tired. She slept until I fed her supper and she went back to sleep. Yesterday she was alright but not so frisky—today she has been playing so much with those old slacks she took off the hydrant in the back yard and big sticks.

We have had a good rain. The sun came out this afternoon and it warmed up. It's been so cold. Garbie stayed in her house while it was raining. She goes out to the fence and runs back and forth, racing with the dog on the other side of the fence. She really likes company.

Garbie is just too sweet. She is kinda "settling down." After she eats, she gets in the house or a cool place and takes a nap. That Garbie is really something!! Yesterday she sang "Tip-Toe Through the Tulips." She only did it one time and I haven't heard her do it since...

That Garbie, she just loves watermelons and cantaloupes. I leave a little of the red melon and she eats it all. Also, Ann gave me some apples off her trees today. I made an apple pie and put it in the freezer. So she got the peelings and cores.

Well I think Garbie has about got all of her stuff brought back in her yard. I have to throw it over the fence out of the way when they mow her yard.

That Garbie, I think her collar is going to have to be changed because she is getting so big. I could do it if she would be still. Alice Long was here and she looked at it and said it isn't too tight. She loves apples. Ann gives me apples off her trees, so I give her some. She loves melons also. I fix Garbie's breakfast, then mine. I always feed her first because she is so sweet.

Today is Garbie's birthday. She is two years old today and still acts like a two-year-old. Yesterday I went to the Food Locker and got her some big bones. I boiled them and she really liked it. I just gave her one. A friend who has a dog and knows more about dogs than I do said it was better for the dog if you boil the bones.

When I gave Garbie her supper it was thundering. I told her it was going to rain and she had better get in her house. So when she finished, she went in her house. We had a hard shower with lots of lightning and thunder.

When I went to town Tuesday, I got plenty of food for Garbie and me. I have been giving her some of my left-over food that I didn't freeze and she really liked the dressing— she eats so fast I don't see how she can taste it.

Garbie is so glad to be home. She put some of the leaves out of her house and fixes it just like she wants it. Thursday night, about 11 P.M., she came out of her house barking and ran to the front gate. When she was satisfied, she came back and went to bed.

Garbie is so funny. When she gets up in the mornings, she yawns, looks all around, shakes herself and goes out in the big yard.

Poor Garbie! She just comes out of her house long enough to eat and back in she goes. She rolls up to sleep so she may be a ball when this winter is over.

One sunshiny day, Garbie was asleep in the sun and about a block away, a boy was on a bicycle in the street. A dog barked at him and awakened Garbie. She jumped up barking and looked all around, trying to decide what she was barking at.

I didn't let Garbie know about the candy you sent—she would have had to have some. I went out in the backyard yesterday to pick up some papers that had blown in and she was so happy. She thought I had come out to play with her and was jumping and trying to run between my legs, etc.

I'm cooking some pinto beans for Garbie and me and heating some homemade frozen soup in the Corningware casserole you gave me for Christmas. It's just the right size.

She enjoys the sunshine. After she ate her breakfast, she hunted a good place to take a nap. Mr. Bass, our neighbor, walks his dog every day and when they pass my yard, Garbie runs up and down the fence with them. She doesn't bark at them—she just wants to play. I think she enjoyed visiting her mother but she is enjoying her house.

I don't know what's the matter with Garbie. Thursday A.M., she looked at her breakfast and went off and sat down. A little later, she ate it all. It was the same thing Friday A.M. but she didn't eat it. I called my neighbor Mrs. Golden and told her. She said her dog did the same thing and she left his food out there. The ants and flies got on it but later he ate it. I poured out the can of Ken L but the Purina Chow she ate later. I told the repairman the way she was doing and he said their dog didn't eat his breakfast that morning. I don't leave Garbie's food out for the flies and ants to get in it. She hasn't been panting since she isn't eating so much.

One day Mr. Bass was working in his garden and Garbie was out there. She reared up on the fence and he was petting her. When anyone comes, she has quit barking at them when I tell her this is our friend. About the golf ball—one day I saw Mr. Bass in his backyard slinging and swinging something around. I decided it was a golf club he was practicing so I guess he hit a ball over the fence and of course, she found it. She might get it lodged in her throat.

Garbie got alright soon after I told you she wouldn't eat. She hangs around the back door looking in to see if I'm going to feed her some more. She is herself again. I think it was the weather and too I was feeding her too much. But you know how she can look at you.

Julio mowed all the yards yesterday. He picked up all the tree limbs and etc. out of his way. After he was gone, Garbie thought it was her job to put them back where they were. Anyway, it gave her something to do.

I have tried to cut down on Garbie's food for she is a little too fat for warm weather just ahead. But I feel sorry for her and throw some Bonz or bread out to her. She is spoiled. She sits at the back door looking.

I love that Garbie, she gets sweeter all the time. I had some dry butter beans so I cooked some for us. She really liked them. I gave her about a cup of them with three cups Purina Puppy Chow. She is always hungry.

My yard is a weed patch; had it mowed last Monday, then again yesterday morning. I'm going to get some weed killer for the front yard but I'm afraid to put it in the backyard because of Garbie—she would have to have some of it. Although the checkerboard man who delivers her food said it wouldn't hurt her, he doesn't know Garbie!

Just a note to give you a report on Garbie and myself. I'm glad to say we are fine and back in our routine again. The vet said Garbie is too fat, which I knew, so I am trying to feed her less. When she finishes, she licks the pan and goes out in the big backyard and eats weeds. Alice said it is alright for her to eat weeds. My foot she stepped on is alright. I washed it good and put some aloe vera on it and it didn't get sore. She tried to clean the blood off that came through my hose. She looked sad about it.

Garbie did the smartest thing last week. The day before this last real cold spell, I took the blue mat out and put it in her house. She was jumping around and so pleased. I told her it was going to get real cold and for her to leave the mat in her house. She took it out before I could get to the door. I took it away from her and got cross with her, repeating what I had told her. She took it out again but I thought I had done what I could even if it didn't do any good. Next morning when I looked out the window at her, she had put that mat in her house all nice and smooth and she was asleep on it. Isn't that smart?

That Garbie! When I washed Monday she took that bath mat, which she loves, and put it over the pipe that the washer water flows out of into the yard. This is the part she has disconnected every time she can. She then sat there watching it as if she was guarding it. Every day that the sun shines, she takes this mat out and puts it in the sun and sits on it.

Soon after you were gone, I went to look out the window to see what Garbie was doing. She was in her house, sound asleep, and didn't come out until suppertime, then she barked until bed time. The people who live in the mobile house across the back fence had a cow and two calves in the yard. She didn't like that a bit.

Last night the ambulance made a run about 11 P.M. Garbie made this mournful noise and wouldn't stop. I talked to her though the window and told her it was alright and etc. for her to go to sleep, so she did. She is so smart.

Garbie is so cute. Yesterday A.M. I slept late. When I looked out she was coming out of her house, looked all around, yawned, smiled, wiggled her tail and went back to bed.

If anybody ever tries to break in, I'll put Garbie's leash on her and bring her through the house and turn her loose on whoever it is.

Karen asked me on her card if I still make gravy for Garbie. I told her yes and I would have to tell her the last smart thing Garbie did. After I gave her supper during the last really cold spell we had, I gave her a new bath mat and told her to put it in her house because it was going to be real cold, etc. She was so pleased. She played with it, throwing it and trying to catch it and tossing it back and forth. In about an hour I looked out the window to see what she was doing and she had put it in her house. It was all smoothed out and she was on it fast asleep. Isn't that smart?

It's been so cold and bad weather after those pretty days. Sunday A.M. I stayed in bed for the 8 o'clock church service, making Garbie's breakfast later than usual, which displeased her. She was pouting with me when I fed her. She was sitting near the fence and didn't come running for her food. When I said good morning beautiful Garbie, she came and was alright. She sat near the door until I took her water and she gave me that droopy look that says, "Is this all you are going to give me?" Then she waddles off to the backyard to tend to her wants.

I think Garbie has fleas again the way she scratches. Did you put that flea powder on her or in her house? I don't know where she gets them.

That Garbie! Several days ago she was playing with a frog—a big frog. I tried to stop her but it was just too much fun. When she came to the door to get a drink, her stomach was jumping like someone with hiccups. After a while it stopped. I think she swallowed that frog plus several golf balls. There were eight balls, then later not so many. At night her dreams don't sound good. She was "jumpy" enough without the frog. She is fat or I would think she was hungry. She still scratches so I use this Hart's flea powder every week. Guess that's enough about her.

Garbie, I had to take her to the vet Monday P.M. I had used flea powder as directed and she seemed to get worse. I called Dr. Metzger and told him about her—thinking—no—hoping he might come by, but no. So I thought of Julio who mows for me. Garbie knows him so he came, put the leash on her and put her in the car. I drove us out there and the doctor was so busy, we had to wait thirty minutes or longer. When he got to her and examined her, he said she has "mange" and fleas and needs to be dipped. I don't know anything about that stuff—that's why I always go to a doctor. I told him to do whatever she needed for she and I were going to be a nervous wreck with all her scratching and talking in her sleep. One night neither of us slept much. Anyway, he gave her a shot to alleviate the fleas and scratching and dipped her. He kept her for one and a half hours and I brought Julio back to town because he had some yards to mow. When I went back for her, the doctor put her in the car and she sat up in the back seat real good. (Ruby drives a 1961 Mercury Comet that has about 20,000 miles on it.) When I drove in my driveway, Alice Long was passing and she sensed something so she put her in the yard for me. She is herself again and I have to mix this solution and put it on her once a week. Alice said she would come and help me with that.

Just a note for you to know Garbie is better but not entirely through with the fleas and "mange." By Monday, which was a week since the doctor had seen her, she was scratching bad again. I was to dip her that day, so Alice Long came to help me with her. We did a pretty good job, went exactly by the instructions. That night she "carried on" all night in her sleep. She would get up and shake herself, etc. But last night, I didn't hear her all night. She has started scratching again. If she gets bad again, I'm going to call the doctor and ask if I can dip her before the week is up, which will be next Monday. This isn't really a "dipping"—the medication is liquid. Just add a tablespoon to a gallon of water, wear rubber gloves and sponge her with a sponge. We put some in her house and took the mats out. This is my first experience with fleas but everybody's animals have them.

I'm still "dipping" Garbie for fleas. She can't go over a week because she gets to scratching so bad. I started several weeks ago treating her on Saturday. She must be better because it lasted only a week this time. She was the sweetest, nicest thing Saturday. I went out in the yard eating a cookie and gave her part of it and told her to let me bathe her and rub her back and she came to me. I talked to her and told her I had some cookies in my pocket. If she would be good, I would give her some more, etc. She didn't like that big yellow sponge so I used a rag. The solution that was left I poured it in her house, which I do every time. She really was good.

I'll bring Garbie home with me Christmas. I can feed her in the utility room if the weather gets too bad for Hazel to come.

I got your letter with the pictures of Garbie and me. She sure didn't look happy. Thank you for sending them. She hasn't been a problem feeding or anything. She didn't want to go out one day. I had a hand towel in my hand and I hit her with it. She rushed out the screen door and looked back—she was so surprised. I felt sorry for her and gave her a bone.

Somebody threw some bones (animal) in my back yard. They were small. Hazel said they are small and look like deer bones. Of course it pleased her, and she brought them to my back door. I wish they wouldn't do that—they might throw something that would make her sick.

Garbie is happy to be home. Hazel feeds her all the time but on pretty days I go to the back door and talk to her and give her a bone biscuit. She nearly wiggles her tail off—she is so sweet. I told them about Garbie crying because she was leaving her mother. She has been just fine, happy, and hungry.

Wish you could have seen Garbie this A.M. At 6:30, she started barking here at her house and my window. I got up to see what it was because she meant business. She was looking at the air conditioner and telling me there was something in it or on it. I couldn't see anything but finally a rat was on my window screen and she couldn't get to it because of the chairs. She carried on until she got so tired she went in her house and went to sleep. I think the rat was asleep on the window screen. It was still there a short while ago when I went back there. I hope something happens to it before bedtime or she will keep us awake all night.

That was Ruby's last letter she felt like writing. After Ruby's funeral service, Garbie was given to Ruby's neighbors who had a teenage daughter. The neighbors had known Ruby for a long time and were pleased to have Garbie.

I hope stories like this will continue to be written about the love of a pet as in this story of Ruby and Garbie.

www.ingramcontent.com/pod-product-compliance
Lightning Source LLC
Chambersburg PA
CBHW040317010626
45792CB00023B/835